Beyond Cash - The Evolution of Digital Payment Systems and the Future of Money

Alex on Finance, Volume 3

Alex Thompson

AF721928

Published by Side Hustle Success, 2023.

While every precaution has been taken in the preparation of this book, the publisher assumes no responsibility for errors or omissions, or for damages resulting from the use of the information contained herein.

BEYOND CASH - THE EVOLUTION OF DIGITAL PAYMENT SYSTEMS AND THE FUTURE OF MONEY

First edition. July 5, 2023.

Copyright © 2023 Alex Thompson.

ISBN: 979-8223468967

Written by Alex Thompson.

Also by Alex Thompson

Alex on Finance

Financial Freedom Roadmap - Achieving Early Retirement through the FIRE Movement
The Art of Strategic Innovation
Beyond Cash - The Evolution of Digital Payment Systems and the Future of Money
Preserving Wealth in Inflationary Times - Strategies for Protecting Your Financial Future

Standalone

Side Hustle Success: Unlocking Your Entrepreneurial Potential
Side Hustle Success: The Ultimate Guide to Passive and Financial Freedom
Mastering the Markets: Advanced Trading Strategies for Success and Ethical Trading Practices
Financial Fortitude

Table of Contents

Introduction:

In today's interconnected and fast-paced world, digital payment systems have become an integral part of our daily lives. Gone are the days when cash was king, and transactions were predominantly carried out through physical currency. The advent of technology has revolutionized the way we pay for goods and services, ushering in an era of convenience, efficiency, and security. This book explores the fascinating journey of the evolution of digital payment systems, as well as the implications for the future of cash.

The shift from cash transactions to digital payments has been driven by several factors, each playing a crucial role in reshaping the way we handle our finances. Firstly, the increasing ubiquity of smartphones and internet connectivity has provided a gateway to a world where transactions can be completed with just a few taps on a screen. With the rise of e-commerce and online shopping, consumers are embracing the convenience of digital payments, transcending geographical boundaries and opening up a myriad of opportunities.

Moreover, the convenience and speed of digital payments have not only transformed the way individuals transact but have also revolutionized the world of commerce. Businesses now have access to a wide range of payment options, enabling them to cater to the diverse preferences of their customers. From mobile wallets to contactless payments, the landscape of digital payments continues to evolve, bringing forth new possibilities and challenges.

The purpose of this book is to delve into the evolution of digital payment systems and explore the intricate web of technologies, innovations, and societal changes that have shaped their development. By examining the historical roots, current trends, and potential future scenarios, we aim to provide a comprehensive understanding of this transformative journey.

The structure of the book is designed to take you on a guided exploration of the topic. We begin with an overview of the rise of digital payments, tracing their origins and early developments in Chapter 1. Chapter 2 focuses on the revolutionary impact of mobile payments, highlighting the emergence of mobile wallets and the key players in the industry. In Chapter 3, we delve into the world of contactless payments and the integration of payment capabilities into the Internet of Things (IoT).

Chapter 4 sheds light on the power of peer-to-peer (P2P) payments, exploring their rise in popularity and the benefits they offer. The subsequent chapter, Chapter 5, delves into the world of cryptocurrencies and the blockchain revolution, unraveling the potential they hold for digital payments. In Chapter 6, we examine the concept of Central Bank Digital Currencies (CBDCs) and their implications for the future of money.

Finally, in Chapter 7, we gaze into the crystal ball and explore the future of digital payment systems, discussing emerging technologies and envisioning the possibilities that lie ahead. The book concludes by reflecting on the significance of adapting to the changing landscape of payments and the potential societal impacts that may arise.

Together, let us embark on this captivating journey through the evolution of digital payment systems and the future of cash. By understanding the past and embracing the present, we can navigate the exciting landscape of digital payments and shape a future where convenience, efficiency, and security converge for the benefit of individuals and economies alike.

Chapter 1: The Rise of Digital Payments

In this chapter, we embark on a historical journey to explore the origins of digital payments and the transformative impact they have had on the way we conduct financial transactions. We delve into the early electronic payment methods that laid the foundation for the digital payment revolution. From there, we witness the game-changing introduction of credit cards and their profound influence on payment systems. Finally, we witness the emergence of online payment systems and the rise of e-commerce, reshaping the landscape of financial transactions.

1.1 Historical overview of early electronic payment methods

The advent of electronic funds transfer (EFT) marked a significant milestone in the evolution of digital payments. EFT refers to the electronic transfer of money from one bank account to another, eliminating the need for physical checks or cash. This innovation revolutionized payment processing by introducing speed, convenience, and increased security.

Early forms of EFT can be traced back to the late 19th century when telegraph companies offered money transfer services. However, it wasn't until the mid-20th century that EFT gained traction with the introduction of computer systems and telecommunications networks.

The birth of electronic payment terminals played a pivotal role in facilitating electronic transactions. These terminals, also known as point-of-sale (POS) terminals, enabled merchants to process payments electronically, thereby eliminating the reliance on traditional paper-based methods. The terminals read magnetic stripe cards, such as credit and debit cards, and facilitated secure and efficient transactions.

Credit cards revolutionized the payment landscape by providing individuals with a convenient and flexible method of making purchases without relying on cash. The introduction of the Diners Club card in the 1950s marked a turning point in the history of payment systems. It was the first card that allowed users to make purchases at various establishments and pay the accumulated balance at a later date.

The widespread adoption of credit cards transformed consumer behavior and propelled the growth of electronic payments. Major credit card issuers, such as Visa, Mastercard, and American Express, emerged, creating networks that facilitated transactions between merchants, cardholders, and issuing banks. These networks established standardized protocols and security measures, ensuring the secure transmission and verification of payment information.

Automated Clearing House (ACH) systems played a vital role in streamlining electronic transfers by enabling the efficient movement of funds between financial institutions. ACH systems act as electronic payment networks that facilitate batch-based transactions, such as direct deposits, bill payments, and electronic checks.

ACH systems revolutionized payment processing by reducing the reliance on paper-based transactions, such as checks, and enabling the electronic transfer of funds. They provided a secure and cost-effective method for businesses, government entities, and individuals to conduct a wide range of financial transactions.

The significance of ACH systems extends beyond domestic transactions. International ACH systems, such as the Single Euro Payments Area (SEPA) in Europe, have been established to facilitate cross-border transfers within specific regions, fostering greater integration and efficiency in global payment systems.

By embracing electronic funds transfer, the adoption of electronic payment terminals, and the establishment of Automated Clearing House systems, the foundation was laid for the digital payment systems we know today. These developments marked the beginning of a transformative journey that would ultimately reshape the way we conduct financial transactions and pave the way for the future of cashless payments.

1.2 Introduction of credit cards and their impact on payment systems

The introduction of the Diners Club card in the 1950s had a revolutionary impact on the payment landscape. It was the first credit card that allowed users to make purchases at various establishments and pay the accumulated balance at a later date. This innovation transformed the way consumers interacted with merchants and paved the way for the widespread adoption of credit cards.

The Diners Club card provided consumers with a convenient and flexible method of payment, eliminating the need to carry cash or write checks for every transaction. Its success paved the way for other credit card issuers, such as American Express and Bank of America, to enter the market and offer similar services.

The widespread adoption of credit cards had a profound influence on consumer behavior. As credit card availability expanded and acceptance by merchants became more common, consumers began to rely heavily on credit cards for their everyday transactions. Credit cards offered a convenient way to make purchases, enabling consumers to buy goods and services even when they didn't have immediate access to funds.

The introduction of credit cards also brought about a change in spending habits. With the ability to defer payment, consumers began to make larger purchases and engage in impulse buying. The availability of credit cards also played a role in driving economic growth by providing individuals with increased purchasing power.

Credit card networks, such as Visa, Mastercard, and American Express, played a crucial role in creating a standardized payment infrastructure. These networks established the rules and protocols that govern the acceptance and processing of credit card transactions. They facilitated the transmission of payment information between merchants, cardholders, and issuing banks, ensuring secure and reliable transactions.

Credit card issuers worked closely with merchants to expand acceptance networks and promote the use of credit cards. They provided financial incentives to merchants, such as lower processing fees and faster settlement times, to encourage acceptance of their cards. By building a vast network of accepting merchants, credit card issuers created a seamless payment experience for consumers, further driving the adoption of credit cards.

The standardized payment infrastructure established by credit card networks and issuers enabled interoperability between different financial institutions, ensuring that cardholders could use their credit cards at various merchants worldwide. This standardization paved the way for the rapid growth of digital payment systems, including online payments and mobile payments, that rely on similar infrastructure and protocols.

By revolutionizing the payment landscape, influencing consumer behavior, and creating a standardized payment infrastructure, credit cards laid the foundation for the digital payment systems we rely on today. The innovations and practices developed during this era continue to shape the evolution of digital payments and drive us toward a cashless future.

1.3 Emergence of online payment systems and e-commerce

The rise of the internet has had a transformative effect on commerce, revolutionizing the way businesses and consumers interact. Online platforms have become the go-to destination for shopping, communication, and information sharing. This digital revolution also brought about significant changes in the way financial transactions are conducted, leading to the emergence of online payment systems and the widespread adoption of e-commerce.

The internet provided a global platform for businesses to showcase their products and services to a vast audience. Consumers, in turn, gained access to a virtually unlimited marketplace, transcending geographical boundaries. This shift in the retail landscape led to a fundamental change in consumer behavior, as more and more people began to embrace the convenience and accessibility of online shopping.

To facilitate secure online transactions, the introduction of online payment gateways played a crucial role. These gateways acted as intermediaries between merchants, customers, and financial institutions, ensuring that payment information was transmitted securely. Online payment gateways enabled the encryption and authentication of sensitive financial data, providing customers with confidence in conducting transactions over the internet.

The impact of e-commerce platforms and marketplaces on digital payments cannot be overstated. Platforms like Amazon, eBay, and Alibaba created a marketplace where merchants and buyers could connect and transact seamlessly. These platforms offered integrated payment solutions, streamlining the checkout process and providing a secure environment for transactions. The convenience, variety, and competitive pricing offered by e-commerce platforms fueled the growth of digital payments and encouraged more consumers to embrace cashless transactions.

Moreover, the emergence of e-commerce platforms also gave rise to alternative payment methods, such as digital wallets and online payment systems like PayPal. These systems allowed users to store their payment information securely and make purchases with just a few clicks. The convenience and ease of use provided by these systems further accelerated the adoption of digital payments.

As e-commerce platforms and marketplaces continue to thrive, digital payments have become the norm for online transactions.

Consumers have grown accustomed to the convenience and security offered by these systems, and businesses have adapted their strategies to meet the evolving needs of the digital economy.

The rise of the internet, the introduction of online payment gateways, and the impact of e-commerce platforms and marketplaces have transformed the way we conduct financial transactions. These developments have laid the groundwork for a future where digital payments are seamlessly integrated into our daily lives, shaping the landscape of commerce and driving us towards a cashless society.

By examining the historical development of digital payment systems, from early electronic methods to the introduction of credit cards and the advent of online payment systems, we gain a deeper understanding of the foundations that have shaped the modern landscape of digital payments. These advancements set the stage for the remarkable transformations that lie ahead in our journey towards a cashless future.

Chapter 2: The Revolution of Mobile Payments

In this chapter, we explore the revolutionary impact of mobile payments and how they have transformed the way we make transactions. We delve into the introduction of mobile wallets and their role in reshaping the payments landscape. Additionally, we examine the key players in the mobile payment industry and the innovative solutions they have brought to the market. Lastly, we discuss the benefits and challenges associated with mobile payments, highlighting the potential they hold for the future of digital transactions.

2.1 Introduction of mobile wallets and their role in transforming payments

Mobile wallets have revolutionized the way we make payments by leveraging the integration of smartphones and secure digital payment technologies. These digital wallets enable users to store their payment information securely and make transactions conveniently through their mobile devices. By replacing physical wallets with virtual ones, mobile wallets have transformed the way we carry out financial transactions.

The concept of mobile wallets involves the installation of dedicated applications on smartphones, which serve as the digital repositories for payment credentials, such as credit card information, bank account details, and even cryptocurrencies. These applications use various security measures, including encryption and biometric authentication, to ensure the safety of the stored information.

Mobile wallets offer unparalleled convenience and accessibility when it comes to making payments. By simply unlocking their smartphones and accessing the mobile wallet application, users can initiate payments in various scenarios, such as in-store purchases, online shopping, peer-to-peer transfers, and even contactless transactions.

The integration of mobile wallets with smartphones allows users to consolidate multiple payment methods in one place, eliminating the need to carry physical cards or cash. This convenience streamlines the payment process and reduces the risk of losing or misplacing traditional payment instruments.

Furthermore, mobile wallets often incorporate features like transaction history, loyalty program integration, and digital receipt storage, providing users with a comprehensive payment management experience. The ability to access payment information, track expenses, and redeem rewards seamlessly adds another layer of convenience and value to mobile wallet users.

Near Field Communication (NFC) technology has played a crucial role in facilitating mobile payments and has become a standard feature in modern smartphones. NFC enables short-range wireless communication between devices, allowing them to exchange data securely and swiftly.

In the context of mobile payments, NFC enables contactless transactions by allowing smartphones to communicate with compatible payment terminals. By simply holding their devices near NFC-enabled payment terminals, users can complete transactions swiftly and securely without the need for physical contact or swiping cards.

The rise of NFC technology has contributed to the widespread adoption of mobile payments, especially in physical retail environments. Its seamless and intuitive nature has transformed the way consumers make payments, making contactless transactions more efficient, hygienic, and convenient.

As a result, NFC-enabled mobile wallets, such as Apple Pay, Google Pay, and Samsung Pay, have gained popularity, with merchants increasingly adopting NFC-enabled payment terminals to cater to the growing demand for contactless payments.

The integration of mobile wallets with NFC technology has not only simplified the payment process but also enhanced security. The encryption and tokenization techniques used in NFC-based transactions ensure that sensitive payment information remains secure during transmission, reducing the risk of unauthorized access or fraud.

The combination of mobile wallets and NFC technology has paved the way for a new era of seamless, secure, and convenient mobile payments. As these technologies continue to evolve, they hold great potential for transforming the way we interact with financial transactions and further driving the adoption of digital payments in our increasingly cashless society.

2.2 Key players in the mobile payment industry and their innovations

Apple Pay, introduced by Apple Inc., has made significant contributions to the mobile payment ecosystem. It enables users to make payments securely and conveniently using their iPhones, Apple Watches, iPads, and Mac computers. Apple Pay utilizes Near Field Communication (NFC) technology for contactless payments, allowing users to simply hold their devices near compatible payment terminals to complete transactions.

Apple Pay enhances security by implementing tokenization, which replaces the actual payment card information with a unique token during the transaction process. This ensures that the user's sensitive financial data is not stored or shared with merchants, reducing the risk of data breaches. Additionally, Apple Pay utilizes biometric authentication, such as Touch ID or Face ID, to verify the user's identity, adding an extra layer of security to transactions.

Google Pay, developed by Google, provides users with a seamless payment experience across various Android devices. It allows users to store their payment cards, loyalty cards, and transit passes in the Google Pay app for easy access and management.

Google Pay supports both NFC-based contactless payments and in-app purchases, allowing users to make payments at physical stores, online merchants, and within mobile apps. The integration with Google's ecosystem enables users to make payments using saved payment information from their Google accounts, reducing the need for manual entry.

Furthermore, Google Pay incorporates Google's advanced security measures, including encryption and tokenization, to protect user data during transactions. The use of biometric authentication, such as fingerprint or face recognition, adds an extra layer of security to the payment process.

Samsung Pay, developed by Samsung Electronics, is known for its unique feature of Magnetic Secure Transmission (MST) technology. This technology allows Samsung Pay to work with both NFC-enabled payment terminals and traditional magnetic stripe card readers, making it compatible with a wider range of payment systems.

By leveraging MST, Samsung Pay users can make payments by simply holding their Samsung devices near magnetic stripe card readers, even if the terminals do not support NFC. This broad compatibility has been a key differentiator for Samsung Pay and has contributed to its widespread acceptance among merchants.

Samsung Pay also incorporates tokenization and biometric authentication for secure transactions, ensuring that users' payment information remains protected. Additionally, Samsung Pay offers features like Samsung Rewards, which provides users with points for eligible transactions that can be redeemed for various rewards.

Apart from Apple Pay, Google Pay, and Samsung Pay, several other players have made significant contributions to the mobile payment ecosystem:

- PayPal: PayPal is a leading digital payment platform that enables users to make online transactions securely. It allows users to link their bank accounts, credit cards, or PayPal balances to facilitate payments. PayPal offers a range of services, including person-to-person transfers, online payments, and even payment processing solutions for businesses.

- Venmo: Venmo, owned by PayPal, is a popular peer-to-peer payment app that allows users to send and receive money easily. Venmo has gained popularity, particularly among younger generations, for its social media-like interface and the ability to split bills, request payments, and make payments to friends or merchants.
- Alipay: Alipay, developed by Ant Group, is a leading mobile payment platform in China. It offers a wide range of services beyond payments, including wealth management, insurance, and even social features. Alipay has played a significant role in China's transition to a cashless society, revolutionizing the way people make transactions and manage their finances.

These players, along with Apple Pay, Google Pay, and Samsung Pay, have shaped the mobile payment landscape through their innovative solutions, secure platforms, and widespread adoption. Their contributions have accelerated the adoption of mobile payments, making them an integral part of our daily lives.

2.3 Benefits and challenges of mobile payments

Mobile payments offer a range of benefits that have contributed to their increasing popularity among consumers. However, they also come with certain challenges that need to be addressed for wider adoption and acceptance. Let's explore these benefits and challenges in detail:

One of the key advantages of mobile payments is their convenience and ease of use. With mobile wallets, users can make payments quickly and efficiently by simply tapping their devices or scanning a QR code. This eliminates the need to carry multiple physical cards or cash, streamlining the payment process and reducing the risk of loss or theft.

Mobile payments prioritize security by employing advanced technologies to protect users' financial information. Tokenization is a technique used by mobile payment platforms to replace sensitive payment card data with unique tokens. These tokens are used during transactions, ensuring that the actual card information is not exposed or stored, reducing the risk of data breaches.

Biometric authentication adds an extra layer of security to mobile payments. Users can authenticate transactions using their fingerprints, facial recognition, or iris scans, making it difficult for unauthorized individuals to access their mobile wallets. This enhances the security of mobile payments, surpassing traditional payment methods that often rely solely on signatures or PINs.

Mobile wallets offer integration with loyalty programs and rewards, enhancing the overall user experience. Users can store and manage their loyalty cards within the mobile wallet app, eliminating the need to carry physical cards. This integration allows for automatic application of discounts, rewards, and special offers, providing added convenience and savings to users during transactions.

Additionally, mobile wallets can track and analyze user spending patterns, allowing businesses to offer personalized rewards and incentives based on individual preferences and behaviors. This targeted approach increases customer engagement and loyalty.

Despite the benefits, the adoption and acceptance of mobile payments still face challenges. One key hurdle is ensuring widespread acceptance by merchants. For mobile payments to be widely adopted, merchants need to upgrade their payment infrastructure to support NFC technology and other mobile payment methods.

Educating merchants about the benefits, security, and ease of mobile payments is crucial to encourage their adoption.

Consumer education is also vital in overcoming the resistance to change and addressing misconceptions about mobile payments. Educating consumers about the convenience, security measures, and potential rewards of mobile payments can help build trust and encourage adoption.

Privacy and data security concerns are important considerations in the mobile payment ecosystem. Users may worry about the collection and storage of their personal and financial information by mobile payment providers. It is crucial for mobile payment platforms to establish robust security measures and transparent privacy policies to address these concerns.

Mobile payment providers should comply with data protection regulations, implement encryption techniques, and provide clear information about data usage and storage practices. Transparent communication and continuous efforts to enhance data security and privacy are essential for building trust and fostering widespread adoption.

By leveraging the convenience, security, integration with loyalty programs, and addressing challenges related to adoption and data security, mobile payments can continue to revolutionize the way we transact. As technology advances and user preferences evolve, mobile payments have the potential to become the primary mode of payment, shaping the future of digital transactions.

The revolution of mobile payments has brought about a paradigm shift in how we conduct transactions. With the introduction of mobile wallets and the innovations from key players in the industry, the way we make payments has become more seamless, secure, and convenient. However, challenges remain, including adoption, acceptance, and concerns regarding privacy and data security. By examining the benefits and challenges associated with mobile payments, we gain a comprehensive understanding of their potential and the impact they may have on the future of digital transactions.

Chapter 3: Contactless Payments and the Internet of Things (IoT)

3.1 Introduction to contactless payment technologies (NFC, RFID)

Contactless payment technologies, such as Near Field Communication (NFC) and Radio Frequency Identification (RFID), have revolutionized the way we make transactions. These technologies enable secure and convenient payments by allowing devices to communicate wirelessly over short distances.

NFC is a short-range wireless technology that enables contactless communication between devices, such as smartphones and payment terminals. By simply tapping or bringing their NFC-enabled devices close to payment terminals, users can initiate transactions swiftly and securely.

RFID technology, on the other hand, uses radio waves to identify and track objects equipped with RFID tags. In the context of contactless payments, RFID technology is often used in cards and tags embedded with payment information. These cards or tags can be quickly scanned by compatible readers, making transactions fast and effortless.

The introduction of contactless payment technologies has significantly enhanced the speed and convenience of transactions, reducing the need for physical contact or card swiping. The simplicity and efficiency of these technologies have contributed to their widespread adoption across various industries, including retail, transportation, and hospitality.

3.2 Integration of payment capabilities into everyday devices (wearables, smart home devices)

As technology continues to evolve, payment capabilities are being integrated into a wide range of everyday devices, expanding the possibilities of contactless payments. Wearable devices, such as smartwatches, fitness trackers, and even smart rings, are now equipped with NFC technology, allowing users to make payments directly from their wearable devices.

The integration of payment capabilities into wearables offers users the convenience of leaving their smartphones or wallets behind while still being able to make transactions. These devices provide a seamless and hands-free payment experience, further simplifying the payment process.

Moreover, smart home devices are also being equipped with payment capabilities, enabling users to make transactions within their homes. Devices like voice-activated speakers and smart displays can be integrated with payment services, allowing users to make purchases or pay for services through voice commands or touchscreens.

The integration of payment capabilities into everyday devices extends the reach of contactless payments, making them more accessible and ingrained in our daily lives. This trend not only enhances convenience but also fosters a more connected and integrated payment ecosystem.

3.3 Implications of the Internet of Things on the future of payments

The Internet of Things (IoT) refers to the network of interconnected devices embedded with sensors, software, and connectivity, allowing them to collect and exchange data. The IoT has significant implications for the future of payments, as it creates a highly interconnected and intelligent ecosystem.

With the IoT, devices can communicate and collaborate to initiate and authorize payments seamlessly. For example, smart refrigerators can detect when certain items are running low and automatically place orders for replenishment, with payments processed in the background. Connected cars can pay for tolls, parking, and fuel without the need for manual transactions.

The IoT also enables contextual payments, where payments are triggered based on specific conditions or events. For instance, wearable devices can initiate payments for public transportation when users tap their devices near a transit gate or trigger payments for digital content or services when users access them on IoT-enabled devices.

Furthermore, the IoT offers opportunities for personalized and targeted marketing. By analyzing data from IoT devices, businesses can gain insights into consumer behavior and preferences, allowing them to deliver tailored offers and incentives. This data-driven approach can enhance customer experiences and drive engagement in the payment ecosystem.

However, as the IoT expands, it also raises concerns about data security, privacy, and interoperability. It is crucial for stakeholders to prioritize robust security measures, implement standardized protocols, and establish clear guidelines to ensure the safe and seamless integration of IoT devices into the payment ecosystem.

The combination of contactless payment technologies and the Internet of Things presents a future where payments are seamlessly integrated into our daily interactions and environments. As more devices become interconnected and payment-enabled, the boundaries between traditional transactions and the digital world continue to blur, propelling us towards a more connected and frictionless payment experience.

Chapter 4: The Power of Peer-to-Peer (P2P) Payments

4.1 Exploring peer-to-peer payment platforms and their popularity

Peer-to-peer payment platforms have gained significant popularity in recent years, transforming the way individuals and businesses transfer money. These platforms allow users to send and receive funds directly from their bank accounts or digital wallets, bypassing traditional intermediaries such as banks or payment processors.

Popular P2P payment platforms, such as Venmo, PayPal, and Cash App, have become widely adopted due to their user-friendly interfaces, ease of use, and social integration features. These platforms leverage mobile applications and online interfaces to facilitate seamless money transfers between individuals, friends, family members, or even businesses.

The rise of P2P payment platforms can be attributed to several factors, including the growing reliance on mobile devices, the desire for instant and convenient transactions, and the shift towards a cashless society. P2P payments provide individuals with a convenient way to split bills, pay back friends, or make purchases without the need for cash or physical cards.

4.2 Benefits of P2P payments for individuals and businesses

P2P payments offer numerous benefits for both individuals and businesses:

4.2.1 Convenience and speed: P2P payments enable instant and hassle-free transactions, eliminating the need for physical cash or checks. Users can make payments or request money with just a few taps on their mobile devices, making it quick and efficient to settle debts or make purchases.

4.2.2 Accessibility and inclusivity: P2P payment platforms are accessible to anyone with a smartphone or internet connection, making it easier for individuals who may not have access to traditional banking services. These platforms provide financial inclusion by allowing users to send and receive money, even without a bank account.

4.2.3 Splitting bills and group payments: P2P payment platforms simplify the process of splitting bills among friends or sharing expenses in group settings. Users can split costs for meals, rent, utilities, or event tickets, reducing the need for cash exchanges or complicated calculations.

4.2.4 Business transactions and e-commerce: P2P payments are increasingly used by businesses, especially small enterprises and independent sellers, as a convenient and secure way to receive payments. These platforms provide businesses with a wider reach, enabling them to accept payments from customers locally and internationally.

4.3 Security and privacy considerations in P2P transactions

While P2P payments offer convenience, it is essential to address security and privacy considerations:

4.3.1 Secure transactions: P2P payment platforms prioritize security by implementing encryption protocols and multi-factor authentication to protect users' financial information. Users should ensure they use reputable platforms and follow best practices, such as using strong passwords and enabling additional security features like fingerprint or facial recognition.

4.3.2 Fraud prevention: P2P payment platforms employ measures to detect and prevent fraudulent activities, such as monitoring transactions for suspicious behavior and enabling user verification processes. Users should be cautious when sharing payment details and should report any suspicious or unauthorized transactions immediately.

4.3.3 Privacy and data protection: P2P payment platforms handle personal and financial data, raising privacy concerns. Users should review privacy policies, understand how their data is collected, used, and shared, and consider platforms with transparent privacy practices and data protection measures.

4.3.4 Dispute resolution: P2P payment platforms typically offer dispute resolution mechanisms to address issues related to transactions. Users should familiarize themselves with the platform's policies and procedures for dispute resolution and act promptly to resolve any payment disputes.

By leveraging the convenience, accessibility, and security features of P2P payment platforms, individuals and businesses can enjoy the benefits of quick and seamless money transfers while taking necessary precautions to protect their financial information and ensure safe transactions.

Chapter 5: Cryptocurrencies and the Blockchain Revolution

5.1 Introduction to cryptocurrencies and blockchain technology

Cryptocurrencies have emerged as a disruptive force in the realm of digital payments, offering a decentralized and secure alternative to traditional financial systems. At the core of cryptocurrencies is blockchain technology, a distributed ledger that records transactions across multiple computers, ensuring transparency, immutability, and security.

Cryptocurrencies, such as Bitcoin, Ethereum, and Ripple, are digital or virtual currencies that use cryptographic techniques to secure transactions and control the creation of new units. Unlike traditional fiat currencies, cryptocurrencies are not issued or regulated by a central authority like a government or central bank.

Blockchain technology, the underlying foundation of cryptocurrencies, is a decentralized and distributed ledger system. It allows participants to record and verify transactions in a transparent and tamper-resistant manner. Each transaction is bundled into a "block" and linked to the previous blocks, creating a chain of information that is difficult to alter or manipulate.

5.2 Analysis of the impact of cryptocurrencies on digital payments

The emergence of cryptocurrencies has had a significant impact on digital payments:

5.2.1 Decentralization and disintermediation: Cryptocurrencies enable peer-to-peer transactions without the need for intermediaries such as banks or payment processors. This disintermediation reduces transaction costs, eliminates the need for third-party approvals, and provides greater control over one's financial assets.

5.2.2 Global accessibility and inclusivity: Cryptocurrencies transcend geographical boundaries and provide access to financial services for the unbanked or underbanked populations. Individuals in regions with limited banking infrastructure can participate in digital payments and store value using cryptocurrencies.

5.2.3 Faster and cheaper cross-border transactions: Traditional cross-border transactions often involve multiple intermediaries and incur high fees and lengthy settlement times. Cryptocurrencies facilitate faster and more cost-effective cross-border transactions, bypassing the need for intermediaries and traditional banking systems.

5.2.4 Enhanced privacy and pseudonymity: Cryptocurrencies offer varying degrees of privacy protection, allowing users to maintain pseudonymous identities and control the disclosure of personal information during transactions. This provides individuals with greater control over their financial privacy.

5.3 Potential benefits and challenges of widespread cryptocurrency adoption

The widespread adoption of cryptocurrencies comes with both potential benefits and challenges:

5.3.1 Benefits:

- Financial inclusion: Cryptocurrencies have the potential to bring financial services to the unbanked and underbanked populations, providing them with access to secure and affordable digital payments.
- Reduced transaction costs: Cryptocurrencies eliminate the need for intermediaries, reducing transaction fees and making microtransactions economically viable.
- Transparency and accountability: Blockchain technology ensures transparency and immutability of transactions, reducing the risk of fraud and providing a verifiable record of financial activities.
- Innovation and financial empowerment: Cryptocurrencies foster innovation in financial services, enabling the development of decentralized applications, smart contracts, and new economic models.

5.3.2 Challenges:

- Volatility and market risks: Cryptocurrencies are known for their price volatility, making them susceptible to speculation and market manipulation. This volatility poses risks for users and businesses, particularly in terms of price stability and value preservation.
- Regulatory and legal concerns: The regulatory landscape for cryptocurrencies is still evolving, and legal frameworks vary across jurisdictions. Uncertainty in regulations can create challenges for businesses and hinder mainstream adoption.
- Scalability and transaction speed: Blockchain scalability remains a challenge, with some cryptocurrencies

experiencing limitations in processing a high volume of transactions quickly. This can lead to delays and congestion within the network.

- Security and fraud risks: While blockchain technology offers robust security, individual users must be cautious about securing their private keys and protecting themselves from hacking, scams, and phishing attempts.
- Environmental impact: The energy consumption associated with certain cryptocurrencies, such as Bitcoin, has raised concerns about their environmental footprint and sustainability.

By understanding the potential benefits and challenges of widespread cryptocurrency adoption, stakeholders can navigate the evolving landscape of digital payments and explore opportunities for innovation while addressing regulatory, security, and scalability considerations.

Chapter 6: Central Bank Digital Currencies (CBDCs)

6.1 Understanding the concept of CBDCs and their purpose

Central Bank Digital Currencies (CBDCs) are digital forms of national fiat currencies issued and regulated by central banks. Unlike cryptocurrencies, which operate independently of central banks, CBDCs are backed by the full faith and credit of the respective governments. CBDCs aim to combine the benefits of digital payments with the stability and trust associated with traditional fiat currencies.

The purpose of CBDCs varies among countries but generally includes:

Central Bank Digital Currencies (CBDCs) are digital forms of national fiat currencies issued and regulated by central banks. Unlike cryptocurrencies, which operate independently of central banks, CBDCs are backed by the full faith and credit of the respective governments. CBDCs aim to combine the benefits of digital payments with the stability and trust associated with traditional fiat currencies.6.2 Examples of countries exploring or implementing CBDCs

One of the primary objectives of CBDCs is to provide access to digital payment services for individuals who may not have access to traditional banking services. By leveraging CBDCs, individuals can participate in the digital economy, conduct transactions, and access financial services without the need for a traditional bank account. CBDCs can help reduce the financial inclusion gap by ensuring that everyone has equal access to digital payments and financial services.

CBDCs have the potential to streamline payment processes and improve payment efficiency. Traditional payment systems often involve intermediaries, resulting in longer settlement times and higher transaction costs. CBDCs can eliminate some of these intermediaries, allowing for faster and more efficient transactions. The use of blockchain or distributed ledger technology in CBDC systems can enhance transparency, security, and traceability, further improving the efficiency of payment systems.

CBDCs provide central banks with greater control and oversight over the monetary system. By issuing a digital version of their national currency, central banks can monitor and manage the flow of money more effectively. CBDCs enable central banks to implement monetary policies, such as adjusting interest rates and managing inflation, in a more precise and timely manner. They also provide central banks with better visibility into financial transactions, aiding in the detection of illicit activities and ensuring compliance with regulations.

The People's Bank of China is leading the development and pilot testing of the Digital Currency Electronic Payment (DCEP), also known as the Digital Yuan. The Chinese government aims to provide a secure, convenient, and efficient means of digital payment while maintaining control over the monetary system.

The Riksbank is exploring the potential issuance of an e-krona, a digital complement to physical cash. The objective is to ensure that the general public continues to have access to a secure means of payment in a digitalized economy.

The Central Bank of The Bahamas has introduced the Sand Dollar, a digital version of the Bahamian dollar. It aims to improve financial inclusion, reduce costs associated with cash handling, and enhance the efficiency of payment systems in the country's archipelago.

The Federal Reserve has been researching and studying the implications of a potential CBDC, often referred to as the digital dollar. The focus is on understanding the benefits, risks, and impact on monetary policy and financial stability.

CBDCs have the potential to provide access to digital payment services to individuals who are unbanked or underbanked. This can lead to increased financial inclusion, allowing more people to participate in the digital economy and access essential financial services.

CBDCs can streamline payment processes, resulting in faster and more efficient transactions. Settlement times can be reduced, and transaction costs can be minimized. This can benefit individuals, businesses, and the overall economy by promoting seamless and frictionless digital payments.

CBDCs may impact the role of traditional financial intermediaries, such as commercial banks and payment processors. With the ability to conduct peer-to-peer transactions using CBDCs, individuals and businesses may have less reliance on intermediaries for payment services. This may require adjustments in business models and a reevaluation of the value proposition for traditional financial institutions.

CBDCs can provide central banks with new tools for implementing monetary policy. The ability to monitor transactions in real-time can provide valuable data and insights into economic trends. Central banks can respond more effectively to changes in the economy and adjust monetary policy measures accordingly.

The implementation of CBDCs raises concerns about privacy and the collection and use of personal and financial data. Striking a balance between transaction privacy and regulatory compliance will be crucial. Robust security measures and privacy safeguards should be in place to protect user data and ensure trust in the CBDC systems.

As central banks continue to explore and develop CBDCs, careful consideration of technological, regulatory, and social factors is necessary. Collaboration between stakeholders, including central banks, regulators, financial institutions, and technology providers, will be essential to navigate the complexities and seize the potential benefits of CBDCs while addressing potential challenges and risks.

Several countries have been actively exploring or implementing CBDCs:

The People's Bank of China is at the forefront of CBDC development with the Digital Currency Electronic Payment (DCEP), also known as the Digital Yuan. China aims to provide a secure, convenient, and efficient means of digital payment while maintaining control over the monetary system. The Digital Yuan is being piloted in various cities and has the potential to transform the way payments are made in China, enhancing financial inclusion and reducing reliance on traditional cash.6.3 Implications of CBDCs on financial systems and digital payments

Sweden's Riksbank is actively exploring the issuance of an e-krona, a digital complement to physical cash. With the rise of cashless transactions and the decreasing use of physical currency in Sweden, the e-krona aims to ensure that the general public continues to have access to a secure means of payment in a digitalized economy. The e-krona project focuses on maintaining public trust, security, and privacy while providing a reliable digital payment option.

The Central Bank of The Bahamas has introduced the Sand Dollar, a digital version of the Bahamian dollar. The Sand Dollar aims to improve financial inclusion by providing a secure, accessible, and cost-effective digital payment solution, especially for residents in the country's archipelago. It addresses challenges associated with cash handling and enhances the efficiency of transactions, particularly in remote areas where access to traditional banking services may be limited.

The Federal Reserve in the United States has been researching and studying the potential implications of a CBDC, commonly referred to as the digital dollar. The objective is to understand the benefits, risks, and impact on monetary policy and financial stability. As the world's largest economy, the United States' exploration of a digital dollar reflects the increasing recognition of the importance of digital payment systems and the potential benefits they can bring.

These examples demonstrate the global interest in CBDCs and the diverse objectives behind their implementation. Each country's approach to CBDCs reflects its unique economic, social, and technological landscape, emphasizing financial inclusion, efficiency, and maintaining monetary control. As CBDC initiatives progress, valuable insights will be gained, shaping the future of digital payments and the financial landscape on a global scale.

The introduction of CBDCs carries various implications for financial systems and digital payments:

One of the key benefits of CBDCs is the potential to increase financial inclusion. By providing access to digital payment services, CBDCs can reach unbanked and underbanked populations who may not have access to traditional banking services. CBDCs can enable individuals to participate in the digital economy, access financial services, and make transactions more easily and securely, reducing the reliance on cash.

CBDC transactions can be recorded on a secure and transparent blockchain or distributed ledger, providing enhanced security and transparency. This can reduce the risks associated with fraud, counterfeiting, and money laundering, as the decentralized nature of the blockchain ensures that transactions are verifiable and tamper-proof. The use of encryption and cryptographic techniques further enhances the security of CBDC transactions, providing individuals and businesses with greater confidence in digital payments.

CBDCs have the potential to reshape the role of traditional financial intermediaries, such as commercial banks and payment processors. With CBDCs issued directly by central banks, the need for intermediaries to facilitate transactions may decrease. This could impact the traditional banking system, requiring financial institutions to adapt their business models and find new ways to provide value-added services to customers. However, it is important to note that even with CBDCs, intermediaries may still play a role in areas such as customer support, value-added services, and financial advisory.

CBDCs can offer central banks new tools for implementing monetary policy. The ability to track and monitor transactions in real-time provides central banks with valuable data and insights into economic trends. This can enable more targeted and effective policy interventions, such as adjusting interest rates, managing inflation, and responding to economic changes. CBDCs can also facilitate the distribution of monetary stimulus directly to individuals and businesses, potentially increasing the speed and effectiveness of monetary policy measures.

The implementation of CBDCs raises concerns about privacy and the collection and use of personal and financial data. Striking a balance between transaction privacy and regulatory compliance is crucial. While CBDCs can offer advantages such as improved traceability and anti-money laundering measures, protecting the privacy of individuals' financial transactions and personal information is of utmost importance. Robust data protection measures, including encryption, anonymization, and strict privacy regulations, must be in place to ensure the privacy and security of CBDC transactions.

As countries continue to explore and develop CBDCs, careful consideration of these implications is necessary. Collaboration between central banks, regulators, financial institutions, and technology providers is vital to ensure that CBDCs are designed and implemented in a way that maximizes their benefits while addressing potential challenges and risks.

As central banks continue to explore and develop CBDCs, it is essential to address technological, regulatory, and social considerations to ensure a smooth transition and maximize the benefits of digital currencies while managing potential risks.

Chapter 7: The Future of Digital Payment Systems

7.1 Emerging technologies shaping the future of payments

7.1.1 Artificial Intelligence (AI) and Machine Learning

Artificial Intelligence (AI) and Machine Learning (ML) technologies are poised to revolutionize digital payment systems. With their ability to analyze vast amounts of transaction data in real-time, AI and ML can significantly improve fraud detection and prevention. By identifying patterns and anomalies, these technologies can quickly flag suspicious activities and help mitigate fraudulent transactions.

Moreover, AI-powered chatbots and virtual assistants are transforming customer support in the digital payment industry. These intelligent systems can handle customer inquiries, provide real-time assistance, and offer personalized recommendations. Through natural language processing and machine learning algorithms, chatbots and virtual assistants can understand customer preferences, anticipate their needs, and offer tailored payment experiences.

7.1.2 Biometrics and Authentication

Biometric authentication methods, such as fingerprint recognition, facial recognition, and iris scanning, have emerged as powerful tools in the realm of digital payments. These technologies harness unique biological characteristics to provide enhanced security and convenience in user authentication.

One of the primary advantages of biometric authentication is its ability to offer a seamless and frictionless user experience. Instead of relying on passwords or PINs that can be forgotten, stolen, or easily guessed, biometric authentication allows individuals to verify their identity through a simple scan or touch. For example, fingerprint recognition utilizes the distinctive patterns on an individual's fingertip, while facial recognition analyzes facial features and contours. Similarly, iris scanning uses the unique patterns within the iris of the eye to establish identity.

By reducing the reliance on traditional authentication methods, such as passwords and PINs, biometric authentication provides a higher level of confidence in verifying user identity. Biometric data is inherently tied to the individual and is difficult to replicate, making it significantly more challenging for unauthorized individuals to gain access to digital payment accounts. This robust level of security helps prevent identity theft, fraud, and unauthorized transactions.

Moreover, biometric authentication methods offer added convenience and speed in the authentication process. Users no longer need to remember and enter complex passwords or PINs repeatedly. Instead, a quick scan or touch of a fingerprint, face, or iris is sufficient to verify their identity. This streamlined authentication process improves the user experience and reduces the risk of human error.

However, it is essential to address concerns related to privacy and data protection in the context of biometric authentication. Collecting and storing biometric data require robust security measures to prevent unauthorized access and misuse. Striking a balance between the convenience and security of biometric authentication while safeguarding user privacy is crucial.

7.1.3 Internet of Things (IoT)

The Internet of Things (IoT) has revolutionized the way we interact with technology, and its integration with digital payment systems opens up a world of possibilities. IoT devices, ranging from smartwatches and smart speakers to household appliances and even vehicles, can now facilitate seamless and context-aware transactions.

The integration of digital payment capabilities into IoT devices enables frictionless transactions, where purchases can be initiated autonomously based on predefined preferences and triggers. For example, a smart refrigerator equipped with payment capabilities can detect when certain items are running low and automatically place an order for restocking. Similarly, a connected car can pay for parking fees or tolls without the need for manual intervention.

This seamless integration of payment capabilities into IoT devices enhances convenience and efficiency for users. It eliminates the need for traditional payment methods, such as cash or credit cards, and simplifies the transaction process. With IoT-enabled payments, individuals can make purchases effortlessly, saving time and reducing friction in their daily lives.

In addition to convenience, IoT devices can leverage blockchain technology to ensure secure and transparent transactions. Blockchain provides a decentralized and immutable ledger that records and verifies transactions. By leveraging blockchain, IoT devices can securely process and record payments, eliminating the need for intermediaries and reducing the risk of fraud or tampering.

Furthermore, the IoT ecosystem enables the emergence of microtransactions, where small payments can be seamlessly executed. For instance, IoT devices can interact with each other and exchange value in real-time, such as a smart parking meter communicating with a vehicle to automatically deduct the parking fee. This opens up opportunities for new business models and revenue streams, as well as innovative use cases where even the smallest transactions can be executed efficiently.

However, it is important to address security and privacy concerns associated with IoT devices. As these devices become more interconnected and handle sensitive financial information, robust security measures must be implemented to protect against unauthorized access, data breaches, and malicious activities. User consent, data encryption, and secure communication protocols are vital to safeguard the privacy and security of IoT-enabled payments.

7.2 Predictions and possibilities for the future of digital payments

The future of digital payment systems holds numerous exciting possibilities:

7.2.1 Seamless and Omnichannel Payments

As digital payment systems continue to evolve, one significant trend that emerges is the shift towards seamless and omnichannel payments. In this era of interconnected devices and diverse customer touchpoints, the payment experience is becoming more integrated, convenient, and consistent across various channels.

Seamless payments refer to the ability to initiate and complete transactions smoothly, without unnecessary hurdles or disruptions.

Whether customers are making purchases online, in-store, or through their mobile devices, they can expect a seamless transition from browsing to checkout. This eliminates friction points in the payment process, streamlining the customer journey and enhancing overall satisfaction.

The concept of omnichannel payments takes this seamless experience a step further. It recognizes that customers interact with businesses through multiple channels, and they expect a consistent payment experience across all touchpoints. Whether they start their shopping journey on a mobile app, continue on a desktop website, or make a purchase in a physical store, customers desire a unified and integrated payment process. This means that their payment preferences, saved payment methods, and transaction history seamlessly transfer between channels, ensuring a seamless and uninterrupted experience.

Enabling seamless and omnichannel payments requires robust technological infrastructure and integration between various systems. Payment service providers, retailers, and financial institutions need to collaborate to ensure that customer data and preferences are synchronized across channels. This allows customers to start a transaction on one platform and complete it on another without any disruptions or the need to re-enter payment information.

Moreover, the rise of digital wallets and mobile payment apps further contributes to the seamless and omnichannel payment experience. These digital payment solutions consolidate multiple payment methods and allow customers to make transactions with a single tap or touch. Whether it's using a mobile device, smartwatch, or even wearable technology, customers can enjoy the convenience of completing transactions quickly and securely across various channels.

By offering seamless and omnichannel payment experiences, businesses can enhance customer satisfaction, improve conversion rates, and build stronger brand loyalty. Customers appreciate the convenience and flexibility of choosing their preferred channels and devices for making payments, and a consistent experience across touchpoints helps to establish trust and reliability.

7.2.2 Tokenization and Digital Identities

In the ever-evolving landscape of digital payment systems, security and privacy are of paramount importance. To address these concerns, tokenization and digital identities are emerging as powerful tools that enhance security, protect sensitive information, and enable secure and verifiable transactions.

Tokenization is a process that replaces sensitive payment information, such as credit card numbers or bank account details, with unique tokens. These tokens are random, alphanumeric codes that hold no value on their own and are useless if intercepted or stolen. Instead of transmitting and storing actual payment data, tokens are used to represent the sensitive information, keeping the original data secure.

The use of tokenization offers several key benefits. First and foremost, it significantly reduces the risk of data breaches and identity theft. Even if a token is compromised, it holds no value or personal information, rendering it useless to potential attackers. This provides a layer of protection for both businesses and customers, ensuring that sensitive payment data remains secure throughout the payment process.

Additionally, tokenization simplifies the compliance with industry standards and regulations, such as the Payment Card Industry Data Security Standard (PCI DSS). By replacing actual payment data with tokens, businesses can reduce their scope of compliance, as the sensitive information is no longer stored or transmitted within their systems. This streamlines the compliance process and minimizes the potential risks and costs associated with data security.

Digital identities, linked to individuals' biometrics or cryptographic keys, play a crucial role in ensuring secure and verifiable transactions. Biometric authentication methods, such as fingerprint recognition, facial recognition, or iris scanning, provide a unique and inherently secure way to verify a person's identity. By linking digital identities to biometric data, individuals can securely authenticate themselves during payment transactions, reducing the risk of unauthorized access or fraud.

Cryptographic keys, such as public-private key pairs, enable secure digital signatures that can validate the authenticity and integrity of transactions. These keys are unique to each individual and can be used to verify the identity of the parties involved in a transaction. By leveraging cryptographic keys, digital identities can be securely established, providing a trusted framework for conducting transactions in the digital realm.

The combination of tokenization and digital identities creates a robust security framework for digital payments. Tokens protect sensitive payment information, while digital identities ensure secure and verifiable transactions. This reduces the risk of identity theft, fraud, and unauthorized access, fostering trust and confidence in the digital payment ecosystem.

As tokenization and digital identities continue to advance, the need for traditional methods of authentication, such as passwords or PINs, may diminish. This shift towards more secure and user-friendly authentication methods enhances the overall payment experience while maintaining a high level of security.

7.2.3 Cross-Border Payments

Cross-border payments have long been associated with challenges such as high costs, slow processing times, and complex procedures. However, the advent of blockchain technology and digital currencies has the potential to revolutionize the landscape of cross-border transactions, making them faster, cheaper, and more transparent than ever before.

Blockchain technology, with its decentralized and immutable nature, offers a secure and efficient platform for cross-border payments. By leveraging blockchain networks, transactions can be executed directly between parties, eliminating the need for intermediaries, such as correspondent banks. This streamlined process reduces processing times and minimizes transaction fees, resulting in faster and more cost-effective cross-border payments.

Moreover, blockchain technology enables enhanced transparency in cross-border transactions. Each transaction recorded on the blockchain is immutable and can be verified by all participants in the network. This transparency helps to combat fraudulent activities and enhances trust between parties involved in the transaction.

Participants can track the progress of their payments in real-time, ensuring greater visibility and accountability throughout the payment process.

Digital currencies, such as cryptocurrencies or central bank digital currencies (CBDCs), also play a significant role in facilitating cross-border payments. These digital assets operate on blockchain networks and offer advantages such as near-instantaneous transactions and reduced reliance on traditional banking systems. Digital currencies can bypass the need for currency conversions and associated fees, enabling efficient and seamless cross-border transactions.

The use of digital currencies in cross-border payments can eliminate the complexities and costs associated with traditional currency exchange. In a digital currency ecosystem, the conversion from one currency to another can be done instantly and at a lower cost, enabling individuals and businesses to transact globally without the limitations of traditional banking systems.

Furthermore, the programmable nature of digital currencies opens up possibilities for innovative cross-border payment solutions. Smart contracts, built on blockchain technology, can automate payment processes and enforce predefined conditions, ensuring the secure and timely execution of cross-border transactions. This automation reduces manual intervention and the potential for human error, further enhancing the efficiency of cross-border payments.

The combined power of blockchain technology and digital currencies holds great potential to transform cross-border payments, making them faster, cheaper, and more transparent. By removing intermediaries, reducing fees, and leveraging decentralized networks, cross-border transactions can be streamlined, benefiting individuals, businesses, and economies worldwide.

However, challenges remain in achieving widespread adoption of blockchain-based cross-border payments. Regulatory frameworks, interoperability between different blockchain networks, and standardization of digital currency protocols are areas that require attention and collaboration among stakeholders.

7.2.4 Peer-to-Peer Payments

Peer-to-peer (P2P) payment systems have gained significant popularity in recent years, revolutionizing the way individuals and businesses transfer funds. These systems enable direct, seamless, and instant transactions between parties, eliminating the need for traditional intermediaries such as banks or payment processors.

The evolution of P2P payments will be driven by emerging technologies, particularly blockchain and cryptocurrencies. Blockchain technology provides a decentralized and secure platform for conducting P2P transactions. By leveraging blockchain networks, P2P payment systems can ensure transparency, immutability, and integrity of transactions, reducing the risk of fraud or manipulation.

Cryptocurrencies, as digital assets operating on blockchain networks, play a crucial role in enabling efficient P2P payments. Cryptocurrencies offer advantages such as near-instantaneous transactions and lower transaction fees compared to traditional payment methods. The use of cryptocurrencies in P2P payments allows for cross-border transactions without the need for currency conversions, simplifying the process and reducing costs.

Furthermore, blockchain-based P2P payment systems can enhance security and privacy. The use of cryptographic algorithms ensures the confidentiality and integrity of transactions, protecting sensitive financial information. Additionally, the decentralized nature of blockchain networks reduces the risk of single points of failure and unauthorized access.

As P2P payment systems continue to evolve, they will offer enhanced features and functionalities. Integration with social media platforms and messaging apps will make P2P payments more accessible and convenient, allowing users to send and receive funds seamlessly within their existing digital ecosystems. Additionally, the integration of biometric authentication methods, such as fingerprint or facial recognition, will provide an extra layer of security and streamline the payment process.

P2P payment systems will also extend beyond individuals and encompass businesses. Small businesses, freelancers, and independent contractors can leverage P2P payment systems to receive payments from clients quickly and securely. The ability to transact directly with customers, without the need for intermediaries, offers businesses greater control over their finances and reduces transaction costs.

However, challenges remain in the widespread adoption of blockchain-based P2P payment systems. Scalability, regulatory frameworks, and user education are areas that need to be addressed to ensure a smooth and efficient transition. Collaborative efforts between technology providers, financial institutions, and regulatory bodies will be essential in establishing a robust and trusted P2P payment ecosystem.

7.3 Balancing innovation, security, and inclusivity in payment systems

As digital payment systems evolve, it is crucial to strike a balance between innovation, security, and inclusivity:

7.3.1 Innovation and User Experience

In the ever-evolving landscape of digital payment systems, innovation plays a critical role in driving the advancement of user experiences and delivering enhanced convenience. As technology continues to evolve, it is essential to prioritize user-centric design principles to ensure that new features and technologies are accessible and intuitive for individuals of all backgrounds and technical capabilities.

One aspect of innovation in digital payment systems is the development of user-friendly interfaces and streamlined processes. The focus should be on simplifying the payment journey, minimizing the number of steps required, and providing clear and concise instructions to users. Intuitive design principles, such as visual cues and straightforward navigation, can significantly improve the user experience and reduce friction during the payment process.

Furthermore, innovation should aim to cater to the diverse needs and preferences of users. Personalization and customization features can allow individuals to tailor their payment experiences according to their preferences, such as choosing preferred payment methods, setting spending limits, or receiving notifications for specific transactions. By empowering users to personalize their payment experiences, digital payment systems can create a sense of ownership and enhance overall satisfaction.

Another area of focus for innovation is the integration of emerging technologies to enhance user experiences. For example, leveraging artificial intelligence and machine learning can enable personalized recommendations, predictive analytics, and intelligent fraud detection. These technologies can analyze user behavior, transaction patterns, and contextual data to provide personalized suggestions and alerts, making the payment experience more efficient and secure.

Moreover, the integration of voice assistants and natural language processing can simplify the payment process for users, allowing them to initiate transactions and access account information using voice commands. Voice-enabled interfaces provide convenience, especially in scenarios where manual input may be cumbersome or inconvenient, such as when driving or multitasking.

Innovation should also address the accessibility and inclusivity of digital payment systems. Considerations should be made to accommodate individuals with disabilities or impairments, ensuring that features such as screen readers, alternative input methods, and appropriate color contrasts are available. By promoting accessibility, digital payment systems can ensure that everyone has equal access to the benefits of digital transactions.

As digital payment systems continue to evolve, it is crucial to strike a balance between innovation and usability. While pushing the boundaries of technology, it is essential to prioritize user experience, ensuring that advancements are not only novel but also meaningful and impactful. User research, usability testing, and continuous feedback loops are vital in understanding user needs and iteratively improving the design and functionality of digital payment systems.

7.3.2 Security and Privacy

In the rapidly evolving landscape of digital payment systems, security and privacy are of utmost importance. As digital payments become more prevalent, it is essential to establish robust security measures to protect user data and financial information. At the same time, it is crucial to maintain a convenient and user-friendly payment experience. Striking a balance between security and user experience is paramount to ensure that payment systems are both secure and convenient.

One aspect of ensuring security in digital payment systems is the implementation of strong encryption protocols. Robust encryption mechanisms help safeguard sensitive data, such as payment card information or personal identification details, during transmission and storage. By encrypting data, payment systems can protect against unauthorized access and mitigate the risk of data breaches or identity theft.

Additionally, the adoption of multi-factor authentication (MFA) can significantly enhance the security of digital payment systems. MFA combines multiple factors, such as passwords, biometrics, or one-time verification codes, to verify the identity of users. By requiring multiple authentication factors, digital payment systems can provide an additional layer of protection against unauthorized access and fraudulent activities.

Regular security audits, vulnerability assessments, and penetration testing are essential to identify and address any potential security weaknesses in payment systems. By conducting thorough assessments, payment service providers can proactively identify vulnerabilities and implement necessary security patches or updates to ensure the ongoing integrity and security of the system.

Another critical aspect of security and privacy is the protection of user data. Payment service providers should adhere to stringent data protection regulations, such as the General Data Protection Regulation (GDPR) or other applicable data privacy laws. Implementing privacy-by-design principles and obtaining user consent for data collection and processing help build trust and maintain transparency in handling user information.

To address evolving security threats, continuous monitoring and threat detection systems should be in place. Real-time monitoring enables the detection of suspicious activities, such as unauthorized access attempts or unusual transaction patterns, allowing prompt action to mitigate potential risks. Machine learning algorithms and anomaly detection techniques can be leveraged to identify patterns indicative of fraudulent activities and take proactive measures to prevent or mitigate potential security breaches.

Education and awareness play a vital role in enhancing security in digital payment systems. Users should be educated about best practices, such as maintaining strong passwords, avoiding phishing scams, and regularly updating their devices and software. Payment service providers should also invest in user education programs to raise awareness about potential security threats and provide guidance on safe payment practices.

Finally, collaboration between payment service providers, industry stakeholders, and regulatory bodies is crucial to establish and enforce security standards and regulations. Sharing best practices, threat intelligence, and collaborating on security initiatives can help strengthen the overall security posture of the digital payment ecosystem.

7.3.3 Financial Inclusion

Efforts should be made to ensure that digital payment systems are inclusive, providing access to individuals who may face barriers, such as limited internet connectivity or lack of financial literacy. Collaboration between stakeholders, including governments, financial institutions, and technology providers, is essential to bridge the digital divide and promote financial inclusion.

By embracing emerging technologies, anticipating future trends, and prioritizing user needs, the future of digital payment systems holds immense potential to revolutionize the way we transact, making payments more seamless, secure, and inclusive.

Conclusion:

In this book, we have explored the evolution of digital payment systems and the future of cash. We delved into the historical development of electronic payment methods, the emergence of credit cards and online payment systems, and the transformative impact of mobile payments. We also examined the rise of contactless payments, the role of cryptocurrencies and blockchain technology, and the potential of central bank digital currencies.

Throughout this journey, we have witnessed the significant shifts in consumer behavior, the advancement of technology, and the changing landscape of financial transactions. Cash, once the dominant form of payment, is gradually being replaced by digital payment systems that offer convenience, security, and enhanced financial inclusion.

As we look towards the future, emerging technologies like AI, biometrics, and the Internet of Things (IoT) are set to further reshape the digital payment landscape. These innovations offer the promise of improved fraud detection, personalized payment experiences, and seamless transactions across various devices and platforms.

However, it is important to consider the potential societal impacts of this transformation. As cash usage declines, there are implications for privacy, data security, and financial exclusion. It is crucial to strike a balance between innovation, security, and inclusivity in digital payment systems. Regulation, collaboration among industry stakeholders, and user education are vital in ensuring that the benefits of digital payments are accessible to all and that user data is protected.

In conclusion, the evolution of digital payment systems has revolutionized the way we conduct financial transactions. The future of cash is uncertain, as the rise of digital payments continues to reshape the way we buy and sell goods and services. Adapting to this changing landscape is crucial for individuals, businesses, and governments alike. Embracing the opportunities presented by digital payment systems while addressing the challenges will pave the way for a more efficient, secure, and inclusive financial ecosystem.

Don't miss out!

Visit the website below and you can sign up to receive emails whenever Alex Thompson publishes a new book. There's no charge and no obligation.

https://books2read.com/r/B-A-FEPY-ZNHLC

BOOKS 2 READ

Connecting independent readers to independent writers.

Also by Alex Thompson

Alex on Finance
Financial Freedom Roadmap - Achieving Early Retirement through the FIRE Movement
The Art of Strategic Innovation
Beyond Cash - The Evolution of Digital Payment Systems and the Future of Money
Preserving Wealth in Inflationary Times - Strategies for Protecting Your Financial Future

Standalone
Side Hustle Success: Unlocking Your Entrepreneurial Potential
Side Hustle Success: The Ultimate Guide to Passive and Financial Freedom
Mastering the Markets: Advanced Trading Strategies for Success and Ethical Trading Practices
Financial Fortitude

www.ingramcontent.com/pod-product-compliance
Lightning Source LLC
LaVergne TN
LVHW090430210926
848480LV00002B/766